MW00886215

This Book Belongs To

I Spy with my little eye something beginning with.......

A Is for

Apple

I spy with my little eye
Something beginning with.......

B Is for

Boots

I spy with my little eye Something beginning with......

C Is for

Corn

I spy with my little eye
Something beginning with.......

D Is for

Deer

I spy with my little eye
Something beginning with......

E Is for Eggplant

I spy with my little eye Something beginning with.......

F Is for

Fox

I spy with my little eye
Something beginning with......

G

Is for

Geese

I spy with my little eye
Something beginning with.......

H Is for

Hedgehog

I spy with my little eye
Something beginning with......

I Is for

Insects

I spy with my little eye
Something beginning with.......

J Is for

Jam

I spy with my little eye
Something beginning with......

I spy with my little eye
Something beginning with.......

L Is for

Leaves

I spy with my little eye
Something beginning with......

M Is for

Mushroom

I spy with my little eye
Something beginning with.......

N Is for

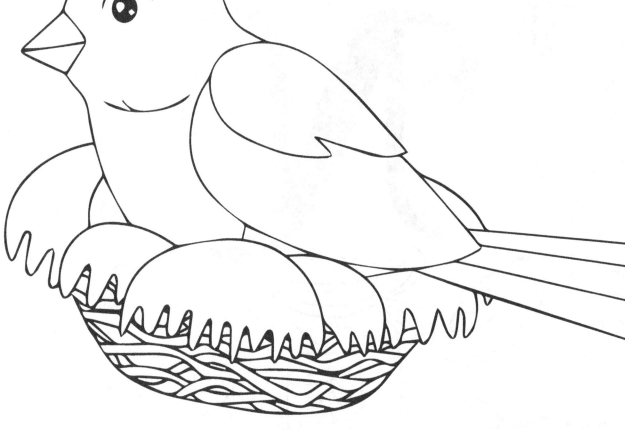

Nest

I spy with my little eye
Something beginning with......

O Is for

Owl

I spy with my little eye
Something beginning with......

I spy with my little eye
Something beginning with.......

Q Is for

Queen Bee

I spy with my little eye
Something beginning with......

R Is for

Rake

I spy with my little eye
Something beginning with.......

S Is for

Scarecrow

I spy with my little eye
Something beginning with.......

T

I spy with my little eye
Something beginning with......

U **Is for**

Umbrella

I spy with my little eye
Something beginning with.......

V Is for

Vegetables

I spy with my little eye
Something beginning with.......

I spy with my little eye Something beginning with.......

X Is for

Ximenia

I spy with my little eye
Something beginning with......

Y Is for

Yarn

I spy with my little eye Something beginning with......

Z Is for

Zucchini

Made in the USA
Las Vegas, NV
07 September 2023

77164676R10031